monday morning®

Super-Duper Science

Outstanding Oceans!

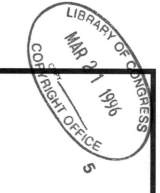

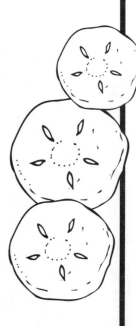

by Annalisa Suid
illustrated by Marilynn G. Barr

For Beau & Jennifer

Publisher: Roberta Suid
Copy Editor: Carol Whiteley
Design & Production: Santa Monica Press
Cover Art: Mike Artell
Educational Consultant: Tanya Lieberman

Also by the author: *Save the Animals!* (MM 1964), *Love the Earth!* (MM 1965), *Learn to Recycle!* (MM 1966), *Sing A Song About Animals* (MM 1987), and *Preschool Connections* (MM 1993).

On-line address: MMBooks@AOL.com

Monday Morning is a registered trademark of
Monday Morning Books, Inc.

Permission is hereby granted to reproduce
student materials in this book for non-commercial
individual or classroom use.

1-878279-91-2

Recycled Paper

Printed in the United States of America

987654321

Contents

Introduction: Why Oceans?

Oceans are outstanding! This amazing environment contains interesting creatures (such as flying fish, anemones, and manatees), a huge variety of plant life, and, on beaches, seashells.

Your students will learn about the exciting ocean world while practicing writing, reading, and speaking skills. They'll learn about tide pools, create reports displayed on mobiles, star(fish) in a musical review . . . and much more. Most of the activities in this book can be simplified for younger students or extended for upper grades. This book will enhance learning in many subjects through exploration of the exciting ocean world.

Outstanding Oceans! is divided into four parts (plus a resource section). **Hands-On Discoveries** contains hands-on activities that allow children to participate in answering science questions they may have, for example, "Who lives inside a seashell?" or "How do tide pools work?" Reproducible sheets have directions written specifically for the children. These sheets are marked with a special seashell icon.

Nonfiction Book Links features speaking, writing, and reporting activities based on nonfiction resources. Most activities are accompanied by helpful handouts that lead children through the research procedure. When research is required, you have the option of letting children look for the facts needed in the library (or in books you've checked out ahead of time). Or they may use the "Super-Duper Fact Cards" located in the resource section at the back of this book. These cards list information for 16 ocean creatures and environments. You can duplicate the cards onto neon-colored paper, laminate them, and cut them out. Then keep the cards in a box for children to choose from when doing their research. These cards also provide an opportunity for younger children to do research by giving them needed information on simple cards.

The **Fiction Book Links** section uses storybooks to introduce information about interesting ocean animals, such as the great white shark. This section's activities, projects, and language extensions help children connect with fictional marine life. Each "Link" also includes a tongue twister. You can challenge children to create their own twisters from the ocean facts they've learned. Also included in this section are decorating suggestions for "setting the stage" for each particular book.

It's Show Time! presents new songs sung to old tunes for putting on a performance. The songs can be duplicated and given to the children. If you want to hold a performance, write each performer's name on the reproducible program page and pass copies out to your audience.

Each of the first three sections ends with a "Super-Duper Project," an activity that uses the information children have learned in the unit. These projects include creating a tide pool diorama, making mobile reports, and writing a treasure chest story. A choral performance is a possible "Super-Duper" ending for the "It's Show Time!" section.

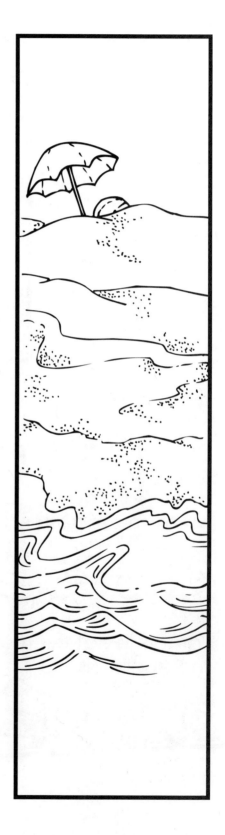

All About Oceans

This is a fish.

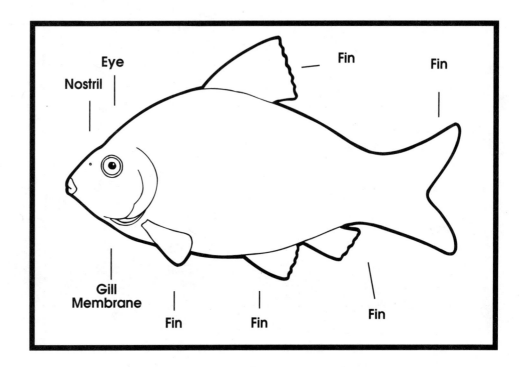

Eye
Nostril
Fin
Fin
Gill Membrane
Fin
Fin
Fin

This is a food chain.

Small fish eat plants, tiny sea animals, and plankton.

Medium-sized fish eat the smaller fish.

Large fish eat the medium-sized fish and the smaller fish.

All About Oceans

Ocean Creatures

A Coral Reef Mural

Corals are tiny animals with soft bodies and tentacles. All produce some sort of outer skeleton to live in. Most live in large colonies. The skeletons of these colonial corals gradually become underwater reefs. Reef-building corals are each about 5 mm long.

Materials:
Tempera paints (blue, black, red, and green), paint-brushes, butcher paper, "Coral Patterns" (p. 9), sponges, scissors, pie tins, newsprint, masking tape

Directions:
1. Use the "Coral Patterns" to cut out shapes from sponges.
2. Pour tempera paint into shallow paint tins.
3. Cover the working area with newsprint.
4. Secure a large sheet of butcher paper to the working area using masking tape.
5. Let the children use the sponges to create a coral reef. Explain that the skeletons of coral build up over time to create a reef. The reefs can grow to be hundreds of feet thick and many hundreds of miles long.
6. Once the mural has dried, post it in the classroom or in a school hallway.

Option:
Children can paint additional sea creatures around the coral reef—including starfish (that feed on the corals) and sharks (that hunt the small fish and shellfish that live in the warm reef waters).

Note:
For more on coral and reefs, children can check out the "Super-Duper Fact Card" (p. 70).

Coral Patterns

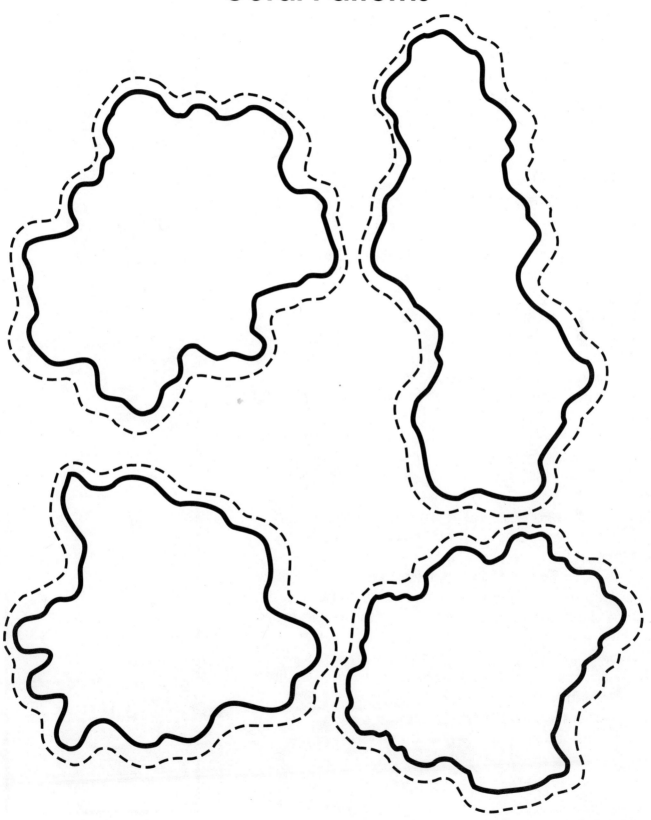

Gelatin Jellyfish

Jellyfish got their name because their insides are very soft, like jelly. If you dived under them, you would see thin, spaghetti-like arms, called tentacles, hanging down. Jellyfish can have a few to a hundred tentacles. Tentacles can be long or short and most of them can cause pain if they come into contact with fish (or people).

Materials:
Flavored gelatin, spaghetti (cooked and chilled), paper plates, "Jelly, Jelly" Hands-on Handout (p. 11)

Directions:
1. Duplicate the Hands-on Handout for each child to study.
2. Make individual servings of gelatin (you can do this in a muffin tin). Follow the directions on the package, making enough for each child in the classroom to have a serving.
3. Give each child a paper plate with a "bowl-shaped" serving of gelatin on it.
4. Set up a working station with bowls of the cooked spaghetti.
5. Let children create their own jellyfish by arranging spaghetti "tentacles" around the gelatin bodies.
6. Have the children look at the different kinds of jellyfish on the Hands-on Handout. Read the names aloud. Let children name their jellyfish creations. They can shake the plates gently to watch the jellies shimmy.

Note:
You can also make sheets of gelatin to cut out with a cookie cutter. Follow the instructions for "Jell-O Jigglers" on the back of most boxes of Jell-O.

Jelly, Jelly

The **comb jelly** is a type of sea jellyfish. It glows in the dark.

The **moon jellyfish** gives off light to attract mates.

The **Portuguese man-of-war** has a sting that can cause a rash that lasts for days.

The **sea-wasp jellyfish** has a sting that can kill a person in less than an hour.

Three Houses for Hermits

Hermit crabs can be found in shallow water pools. These crabs do not have hard outer shells of their own, like most crabs do. They have to adopt shells left by other animals as portable protective shelters. As they grow, the crabs discard their shells and search for bigger homes.

Materials:

"Hermits and Their Homes Patterns" (p. 13), nut cups, small paper cups, large paper cups, assorted decorative materials (uncooked shell-shaped pasta, Cheerios, colored sand), glue, modeling clay or playdough

Directions:

1. Duplicate the "Hermits and Their Homes Patterns" for each child to observe. (Children can color in the crabs and the shells, if they'd like.)
2. Discuss the fact that hermit crabs move to new homes when they grow too big for their borrowed shells.
3. Provide modeling clay or playdough for children to use to fashion a small hermit crab.
4. Let children decorate the nut cups to use as their hermit crab's first house.
5. Have the children set their crab in the nut cup "shell."
6. Have the children add more clay to their hermit crab, until it is too big for its house.
7. Let children decorate the small cups for their crabs' second houses, and place their crabs inside.
8. Have the children add more clay to their crabs until they are too big for the small houses.
9. Children can make very big shells from decorated large paper cups. These will be their crabs' final houses.

Option:

Display the hermit crabs in their homes. Cover a table with blue construction paper and a green crepe-paper "seaweed" border.

Hermits and Their Homes Patterns

Paper Plate Oysters

Some mollusks, such as oysters, are bivalves. This means that their shells have two halves joined by an elastic ligament and held together by strong muscles.

Materials
"Bivalves Pattern" (p. 15), paper plates (two per child), tempera paint (in a variety of colors), crayons or markers, paintbrushes, marbles (one per child), glue, clear packing tape, crepe paper (green and blue)

Directions:
1. Explain that some shells, such as oysters, are called "bivalves." Describe what this means. Children who have visited the beach may have found halves of bivalves before.
2. Duplicate the "Bivalves Pattern" for children to study. They can color the pictures using colored crayons or markers if they'd like.
3. Give each child two paper plates to use to make an oyster. Children can decorate the insides and the outsides of their plates with tempera paint.
4. Let each child glue a marble on the inside of one of the plates.
5. Help children attach their plates with a "hinge" of clear packing tape.
6. Let children help you set up an oyster bed with blue and green crepe paper "seaweed" on a low table. Place the oysters on the seaweed bed.

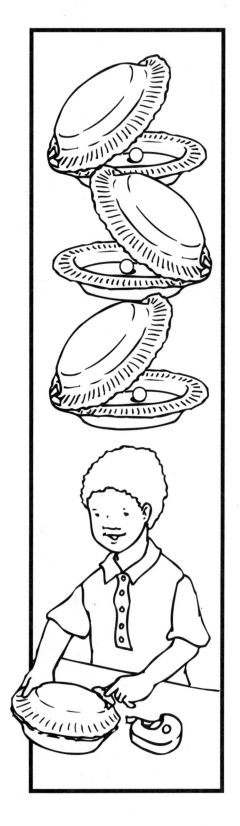

Bivalves Pattern

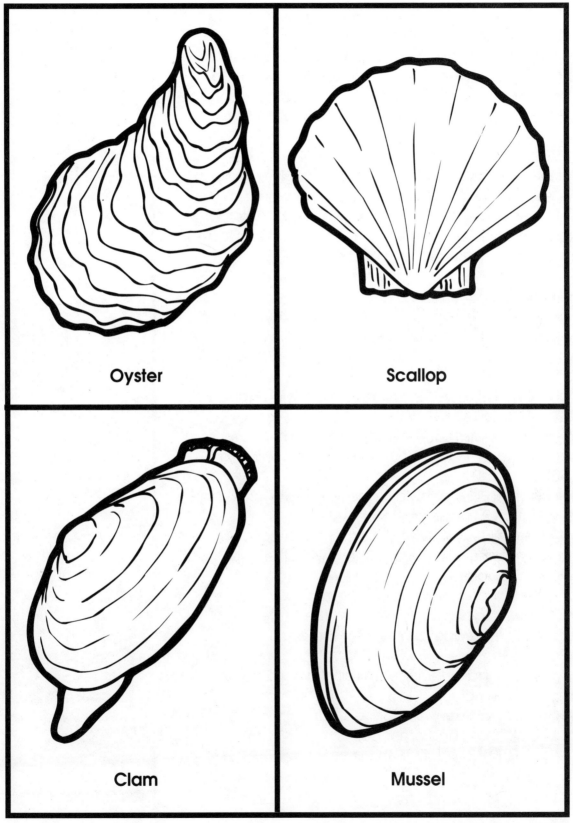

Oyster

Scallop

Clam

Mussel

Papier-Mâché Pearls

Beautiful and valuable, pearls actually begin their lives as an irritant to the creatures that make them. When a tiny piece of rock or sand gets trapped between the mantle of a mollusk and its shell, the animal covers the object with layers of shelly material. This creates a pearl.

Materials:
"Giant Clam Pearl" Hands-on Handout (p. 17), pebbles, papier-mâché materials (strips of newsprint, flour and water mixture), tempera paint (in a variety of colors), paintbrushes, two aluminum "turkey pans," clear packing tape, crepe paper (green and blue)

Directions:
1. Create a "giant clam" from the two "turkey pans" by adding hinges of clear packing tape. Set the clam on a low table, surrounded by a bed of crepe paper "seaweed."
2. Duplicate the "Giant Clam Pearl" Hands-on Handout for children to follow.
3. Tell your students that they will be creating pearls for the giant clam. (The largest clam on record was more than 500 pounds!)
4. Give each child a pebble (or have children scout for pebbles outside) to use as a base.
5. Show the children how to dip strips of newsprint into the papier-mâché solution and then wrap the strips around the pebbles.
6. When the children have completed creating round, pearl shapes (which might be the size of a golf ball or up to grapefruit size), set the pearls aside to dry.
7. Children can paint their pearls using a variety of tempera paint colors. Most pearls we see are white, but they actually are formed naturally in black, pink, blue, and other colors.
8. Store the finished pearls in the giant clam.

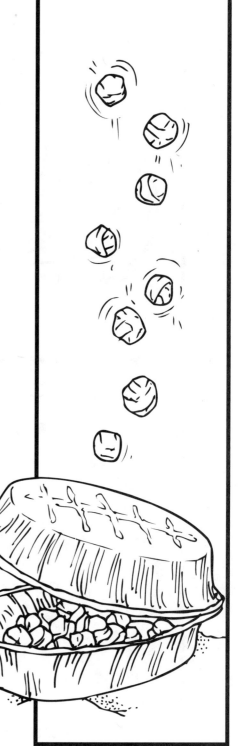

Giant Clam Pearl

What You Need:

What You Do:
1. Pretend you are a clam. A small piece of rock or sand has gotten into your shell. You need to cover it with "shelly" material so it doesn't poke at you.
2. Find a small rock or pebble.
3. Cover the pebble with strips of newspaper dipped in the flour/water paste.
4. Layer the strips until your pearl is the size you want.
5. Let the pearl dry.
6. Paint your pearl.

Oil Slick Experiment

When the Exxon-Valdez hit an underwater reef, 11 million gallons of oil were spilled. The dark liquid stuck to birds' feathers and the bodies of fish, shrimp, and crabs.

Materials:
"Slippery When Wet" Hands-on Handout (p. 19), water, salad oil, plastic dishpan, objects that will float (such as wine corks, plastic film canisters with lids, and plastic lids from juice containers), wooden or plastic stirrers, measuring cup

Directions:
1. Fill the dishpan approximately half full of water.
2. Have the children observe while you pour approximately one cup of oil into the water. Have them make predictions about what will happen to the objects.
3. Have the children watch the oil and see what happens. They can use the "Slippery When Wet" Hands-on Handout to record their observations.
4. Provide assorted objects for children to float in the water.
5. Have them fish out the objects and describe their findings on their handouts.
6. Discuss what might happen to animals covered with oil.

Note:
This observation may be done individually or in small groups. Give each child (or group) a container with a tight-fitting lid. Let the children add the water and the oil, shake the container, and observe the reaction. For a neat effect, add blue food coloring to the water.

Slippery When Wet

1. Does the oil mix with the water?

_____

2. If you stir the oil and the water, what happens?

_____

_____

3. What happens to objects that you place in the water? How do the objects feel when you take them out? _____

_____

_____

_____

4. What do you think would happen if a fish or animal was living in the water when you added the oil? _____

_____

_____

_____

Tide Pool Diorama

Tide pools are homes to many kinds of plants and animals. When the tide comes in each day, it washes fresh water, plants, and animals into the tide pools.

Materials:
"Terrific Tide Pool" Hands-on Handout (p. 21), "Tide Pool Patterns" (pp. 22-23), cardboard boxes (one per child), scissors, yarn or string, hole punch, tape, crayons or markers, pens or pencils, blue cellophane, colored sand, shell-shaped pasta, colored crepe and tissue paper, glue, plain paper (optional)

Directions:
1. Give each child a cardboard box to use to create a tide pool. These boxes can be of varying sizes, from shoe boxes to larger, produce-style boxes.
2. Duplicate the "Terrific Tide Pool" Hands-on Handout and the "Tide Pool Patterns" and give a set to each child to color and cut out.
3. Children can label the patterns on the back. They can write facts on a separate piece of paper and attach to the box. For facts about tide pools, duplicate the "Super-Duper Fact Card" (p. 77) for children to study. Or have children work in the library to research facts from books listed in "Nonfiction Resources."
4. Show children how to punch a hole in the top of each pattern and thread through with a length of yarn.
5. With the boxes turned on their sides, children can tape the free end of the yarn to the inside top of the box. (The pattern will then dangle from the string.)
6. Children can use a variety of materials to further decorate their tide pools: colored sand, shell-shaped pasta, colored crepe and tissue paper.
7. Help children tape sheets of blue cellophane over their tide pools. Tape only one side down, so that the cellophane may be lifted up.

Note:
Children can work together to create a single tide pool.

Terrific Tide Pool

What You Need:

What You Do:
1. Color and cut out the tide pool patterns.
2. Label each pattern on the back.
3. Punch a hole in each pattern.
4. Thread a piece of yarn through the hole.
5. Tape the free end of the yarn to the inside top of your box.
6. Decorate the inside and outside of the box using colored sand, shell-shaped pasta, and colored crepe and tissue paper.

Tide Pool Patterns

Seaweed

Stone crab

Barnacle

Sea anemone

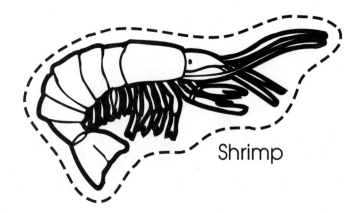

Shrimp

Tide Pool Patterns

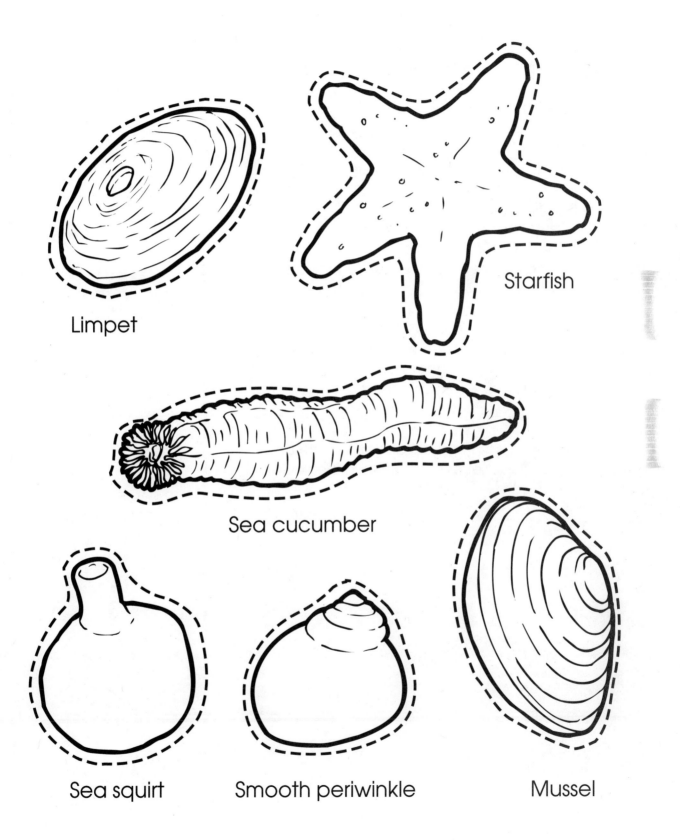

Limpet

Starfish

Sea cucumber

Sea squirt

Smooth periwinkle

Mussel

Ocean Glossaries

Materials:

"Ocean Glossary" Hands-on Handouts (pp. 25-26), writing paper, pens or pencils, dictionaries, construction paper, stapler, glue, scissors

Directions:

1. Duplicate the glossary pages, making one sheet for each child. Explain that a glossary is a list of special words with definitions.
2. Have children look up each word in the dictionary.
3. Children should write the definition next to the word to create their own ocean glossaries. Younger children can draw a picture.
4. As children learn new sea-faring words (or phrases), have them add them to their ocean glossaries.
5. Provide construction paper and a stapler for children to use to bind their pages together. They can decorate the cover of the book with duplicated seashell cutouts.

Option:

White-out the words in the shells and duplicate one page for each child. Let children write in their own ocean-related words and definitions.

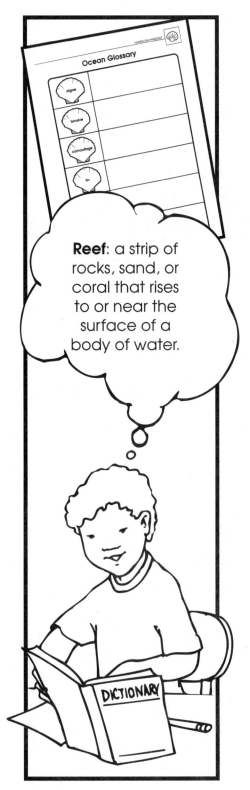

Reef: a strip of rocks, sand, or coral that rises to or near the surface of a body of water.

Ocean Glossary

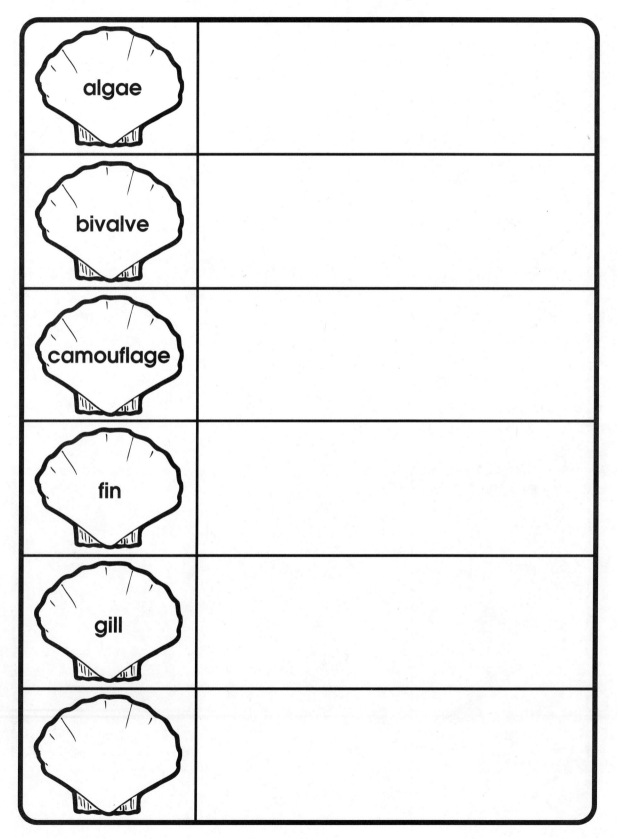

algae	
bivalve	
camouflage	
fin	
gill	

Ocean Glossary

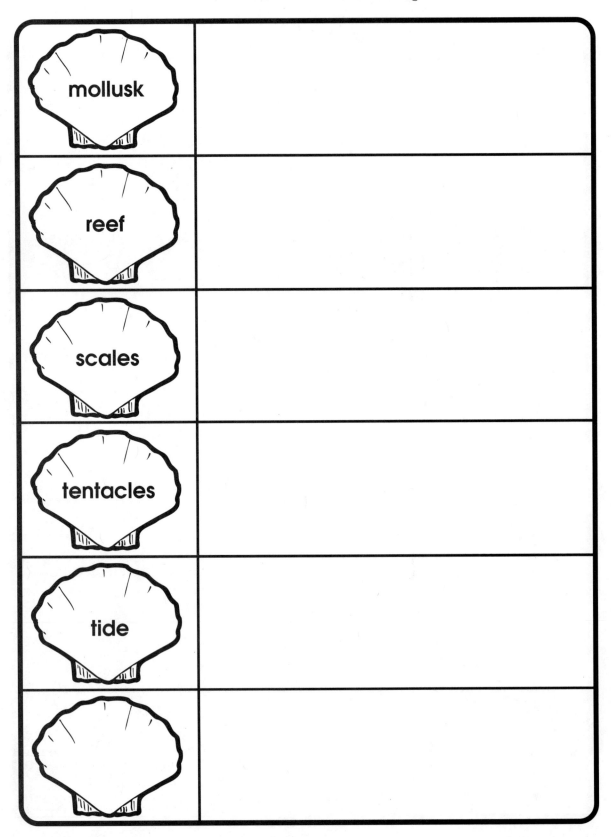

mollusk

reef

scales

tentacles

tide

Creative Coral

Materials:

"Cool Coral Patterns" (p. 28), nonfiction books on coral (see "Nonfiction Resources," p. 79), construction paper (white and black), watercolors, straws, scissors, glue

Directions:

1. Duplicate the "Cool Coral Patterns" for children to look at. Children can further research the different types of corals using books listed in the "Nonfiction Resources" section at the back of this book.

2. Show children how to dot a bit of watercolor onto the white paper and then use a straw to blow the color out in "rays."

3. Let children use a variety of colors, explaining that corals come in many colors, including black, red, blue, and green.

4. Have the children make their own shapes with the straws.

5. Once they have finished their pictures, children can create descriptive names for their corals based on the shapes and colors they've used.

6. For mounting purposes, have children cut out their coral shapes and glue them onto black backgrounds. Post the completed pictures on a "Cool Coral" bulletin board.

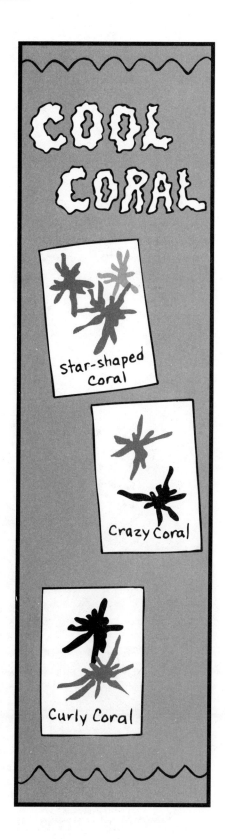

Cool Coral Patterns

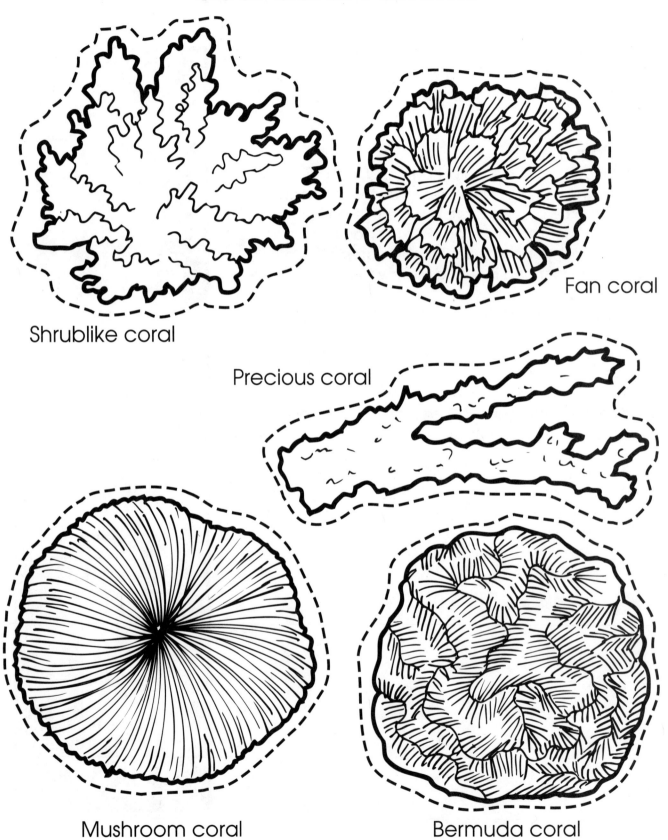

Shrublike coral

Fan coral

Precious coral

Mushroom coral

Bermuda coral

Pearls of Wisdom

Pearls come in all shapes and sizes. Pearls are made when a tiny rock or piece of sand becomes wrapped in shell-like material. The largest pearl in the world weighed 15 pounds. (It was taken from a giant clam!)

Materials:

"Pearl Patterns" (p. 31), "Pearls of Wisdom" Hands-on Handout (p. 30), other pearl books (see "Nonfiction Resources" at the back of the book), scissors, silver or opalescent glitter, glue, pens, hole punch, yarn (white or silver) or paper clips, crayons or markers

Directions:

1. Duplicate the "Pearl Patterns" and cut out. Give one to each child.
2. Let children research pearls, either in books from "Nonfiction Resources" or on the "Pearls of Wisdom" Hands-on Handout. Children can color in the pearls on the handout using the correct colors of markers and crayons.
3. Have children write their favorite fact on the pearl pattern.
4. Provide assorted materials (including glitter) for children to use to decorate their pearl patterns.
5. Once the pearls have dried, show children how to punch two holes in their patterns.
6. Help children string all of the pearl patterns together to make one long "necklace" using yarn or paper clips. Display this in your classroom.

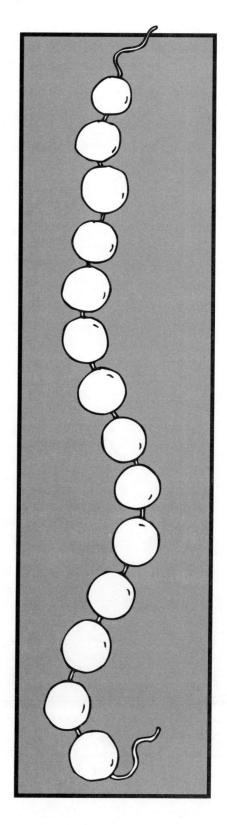

Pearls of Wisdom

What You Need:

What You Do:
1. Write your favorite fact on a pearl pattern.
2. Decorate with glitter and markers.
3. Punch two holes in your pattern.

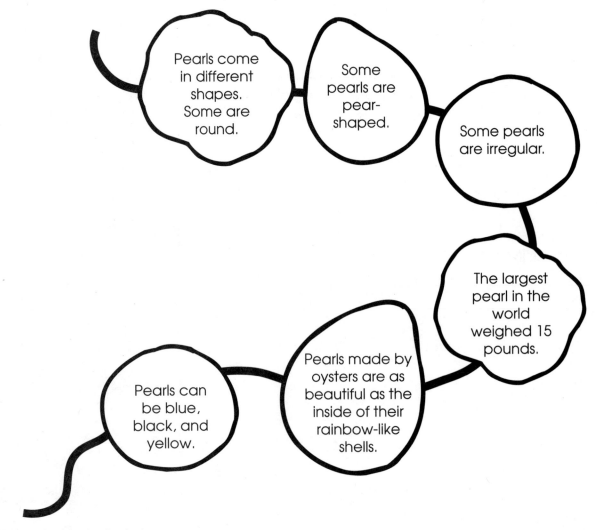

Pearls come in different shapes. Some are round.

Some pearls are pear-shaped.

Some pearls are irregular.

The largest pearl in the world weighed 15 pounds.

Pearls made by oysters are as beautiful as the inside of their rainbow-like shells.

Pearls can be blue, black, and yellow.

Pearl Patterns

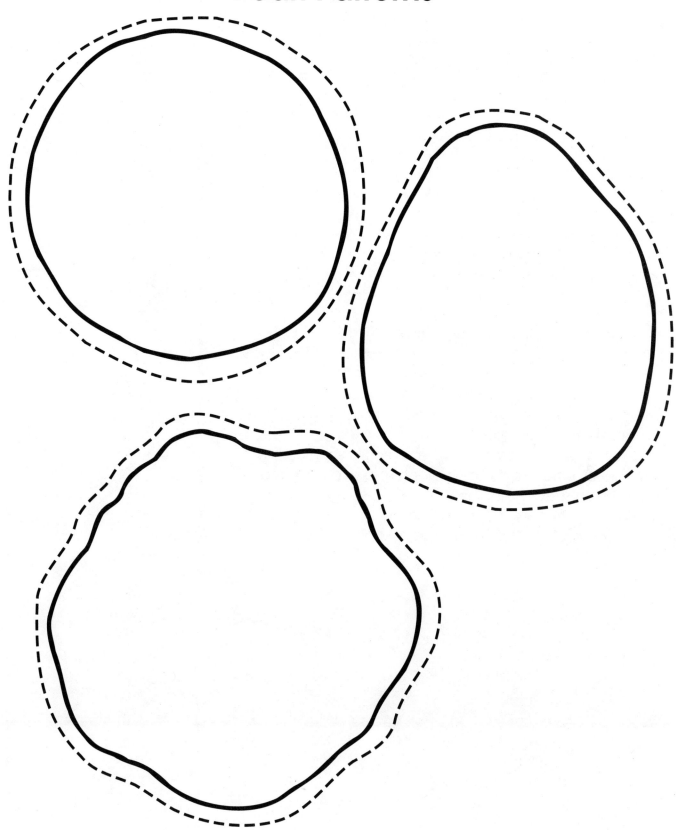

Shark's Mouth

Materials:

"Shark Tooth Pattern" (p. 33), "Super-Duper Fact Card" on sharks (p. 76), butcher paper, scissors, red construction paper, oaktag or heavy cream-colored paper, pencils, silver glitter, glue, newsprint

Directions:

1. Cut a large oval from red construction paper.
2. Duplicate the "Shark Tooth Pattern" onto the oaktag or heavy paper. Make one for each child.
3. Have children write a fact about sharks on the tooth patterns. They can choose their fact from the "Super-Duper Fact Card" on sharks, or by researching sharks in books found in the "Nonfiction Resources."
4. Have the children decorate their tooth shapes using silver glitter and glue. Children can make designs on their shapes by squeezing a pattern onto the tooth, sprinkling on the glitter, and then shaking excess off. (This part of the activity should be done over newsprint to catch the extra glitter.)
5. Once the teeth are dry, have the children glue the shapes around the inside border of the oval, with the sharp points facing in.
6. Post your hungry shark's mouth on a bulletin board or hang it from a clothesline in the classroom.

Shark Tooth Pattern

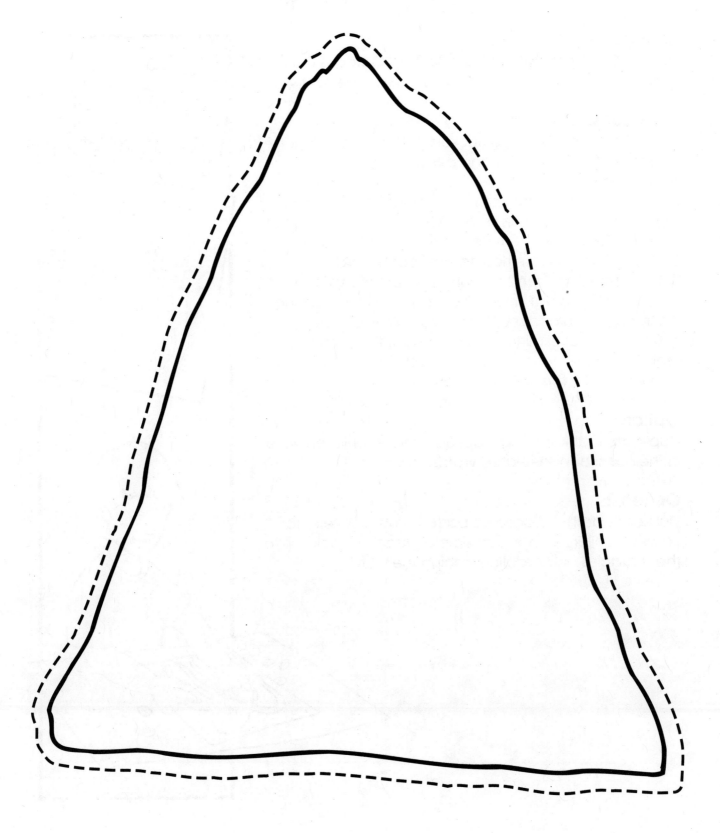

A Spelling "Sea"

Materials:

"Spelling Suckers Patterns"(pp. 35-36), "Octopus Pattern" (p. 37), scissors, crayons or markers, tape or glue

Directions:

1. Duplicate the "Spelling Suckers Patterns," making one sheet for each child and a few extra sheets for teacher use.
2. Enlarge and duplicate the "Octopus Pattern," color, and post on the bulletin board. Cut out one extra set of "suckers" and post them on the octopus's tentacles.
3. Have children learn how to spell each word.
4. Host a spelling "sea" in your classroom. Keep one set of "suckers" in a hat and pull out one at a time, asking each child in turn to spell the word on the pattern.
5. By process of elimination, continue with the spelling "sea." (Children who misspell a word sit down. The rest continue to try to spell the words.)

Option 1:

Duplicate blank spelling "suckers" and let children write in their own ocean-related words.

Option 2:

Duplicate both the octopus pattern and "suckers" for younger children. They can simply tape the "suckers" to the tentacles and practice tracing the words.

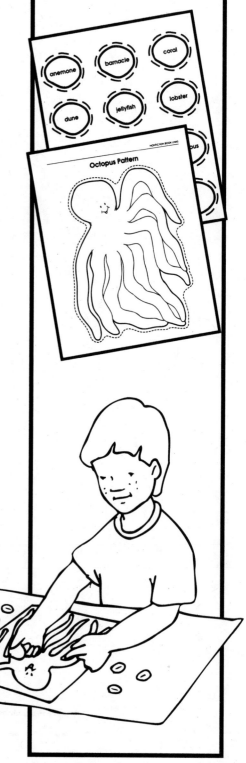

Spelling Suckers Patterns

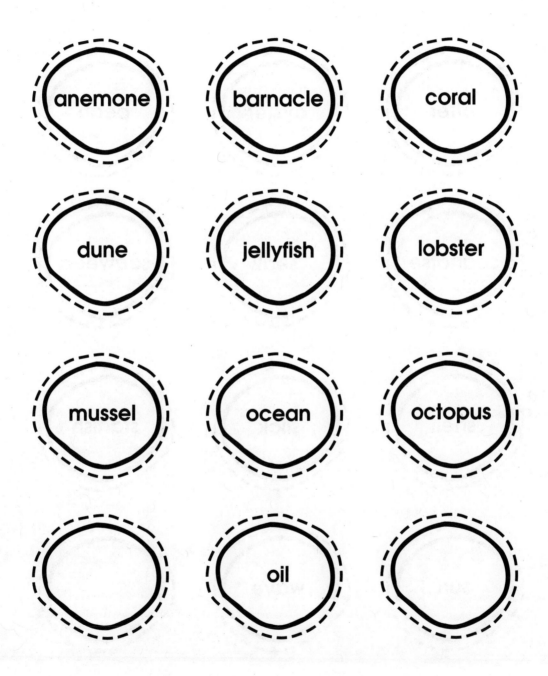

Spelling Suckers Patterns

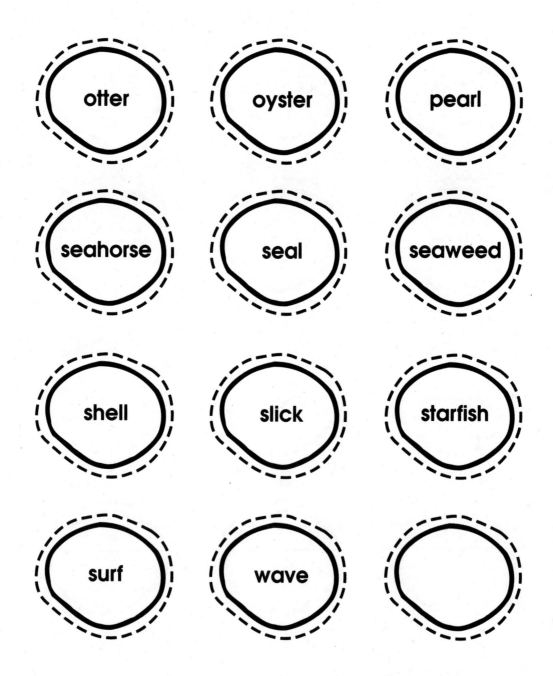

Octopus Pattern

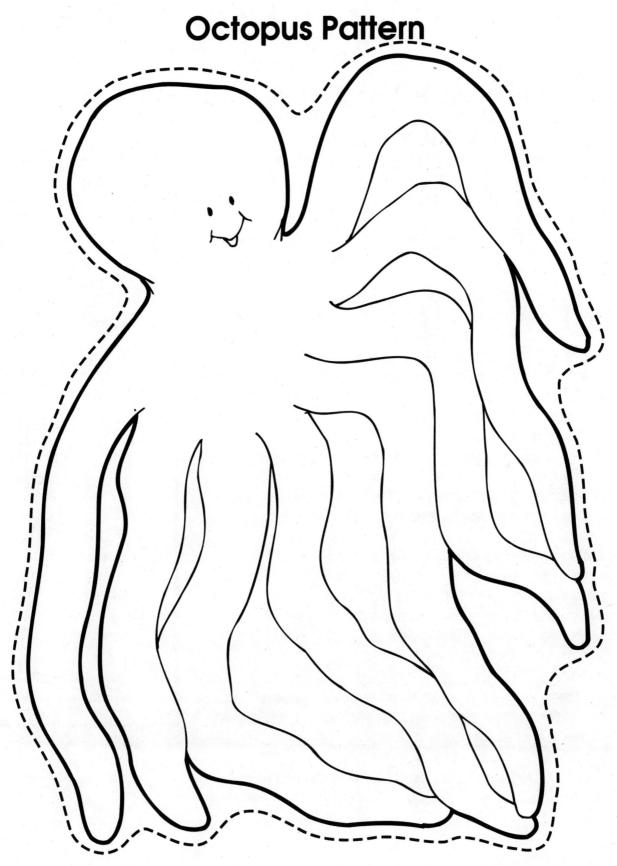

Interview with an Ocean Creature

Materials:

"Ocean Creature Fact Sheet" Hands-on Handout (p. 39), "Ocean Creature Interview Sheet" Hands-on Handout (p. 40), "Super-Duper Fact Cards" (pp. 70-77), writing materials, other books from the "Nonfiction Resources" list (p. 79)

Directions:

1. In these reports, children research ocean dwellers and then play the part of those creatures in an interview setting.

2. Let each child choose an animal, fish, or plant to research. The children can choose from the "Ocean A to Z List" (p. 78). Children can use the "Super-Duper Fact Cards" at the end of the book to research their subjects. Or they can use books from the library.

3. Duplicate the "Ocean Creature Fact Sheet" Hands-on Handout and the "Ocean Creature Interview Sheet" Hands-on Handout.

4. Have the children research their chosen creature using the guidelines on the "Ocean Creature Fact Sheet" Hands-on Handout. Then have them write questions based on the facts using the "Interview Sheet" Hands-on Handout.

5. Once the children have finished their research, divide them into pairs. Each partner will take a turn interviewing the other in front of the class.

6. Set up an interview schedule, perhaps working through five to six interviews per day.

Options:

- Children can dress up to look like their chosen creatures, for example, a child pretending to be a clownfish could dress in many colors.
- Interviewers can hold simple microphones (cardboard tubes with egg carton sections glued to the top).

Ocean Creature Fact Sheet

Use this fact sheet to record at least four facts about your chosen creature. (Remember to list the books you use.) You can use the back of this sheet if you need more room.

My name is: _____

My ocean creature is: _____

Fact: _____

_____

Fact: _____

_____

Fact: _____

_____

Fact: _____

_____

Books I used:

Title: _____

Author: _____

Title: _____

Author: _____

Ocean Creature Interview Sheet

Write your answers under the questions. Write your own question for question 5. Your partner will use these questions to interview you in front of the class.

Question 1: What kind of creature are you?

_____

_____

Question 2: Where do you live?

_____

_____

Question 3: What enemies do you have?

_____

_____

Question 4: What do you eat?

_____

_____

Question 5:

_____

_____

Paper Bag Anemones

Anemones are known as the "flowers" of the shore. Their beautiful coloring makes them look very touchable. However, the "petals" are actually poisonous tentacles. When an unfortunate small fish or other creature brushes against the anemone, its tentacles flick out and attack! Certain fish, such as clownfish, are protected by the anemones. These fish help the anemones by acting as bait to lure other fish to the anemone.

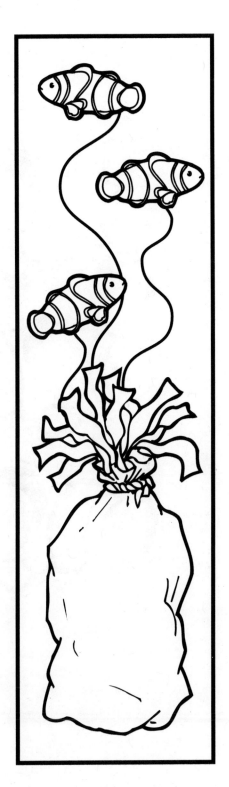

Materials:

Small paper lunch bags, tempera paint, paintbrushes, newsprint, tissue paper, "Clownfish Patterns" (p. 42), "Amazing Anemones Patterns" (p. 43), yarn, "Super-Duper Fact Card" on sea anemones (p. 74), other nonfiction resources on anemones, markers or crayons, pens or pencils, scissors, glue, tape or stapler

Directions:

1. Duplicate the page of "Clownfish Patterns" for each child to color (on one side) and cut out.
2. Duplicate the "Super-Duper Fact Card" on sea anemones and the "Amazing Anemones Patterns" for each child to study.
3. Show children how to make anemones from the paper bags. They can paint the bags with tempera paint. Once the paint has dried, they can stuff the bags with newsprint and tie the neck of the bags with yarn.
4. Provide tissue paper for children to use to cut into strips and glue to the neck of the bags for tentacles.
5. Have children write one anemone fact on each of the clownfish patterns.
6. Show children how to attach the clownfish to the tentacles with tape (or staples).
7. Display a "garden" of anemones on a low table. Observers can carefully lift the fish and read the facts on the back.

Clownfish Patterns

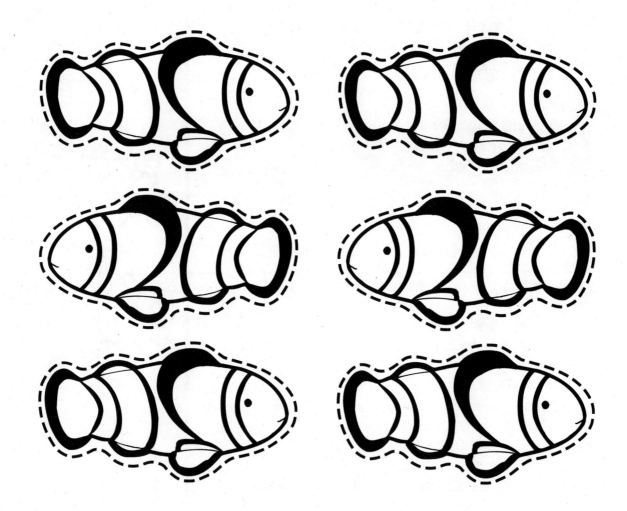

Amazing Anemones

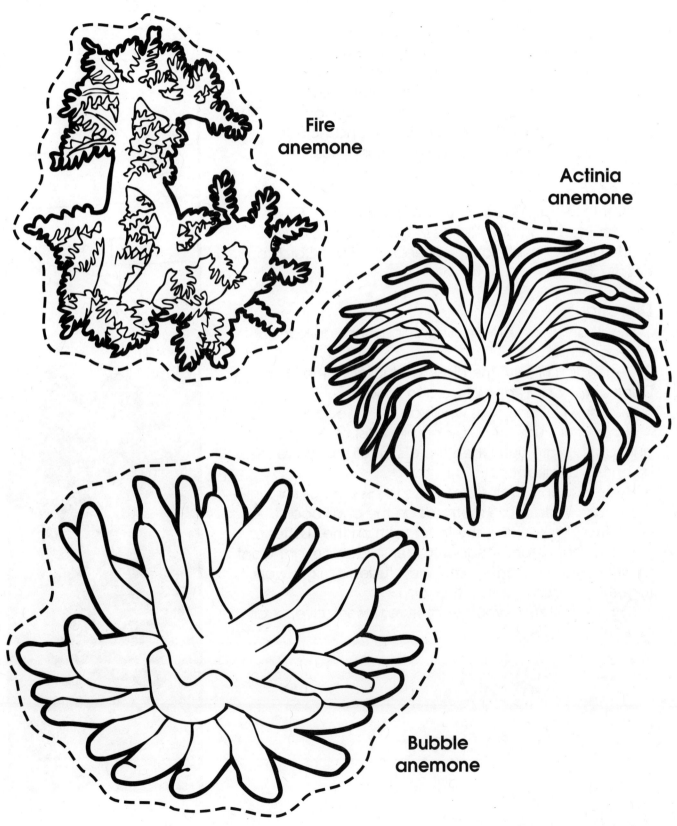

Fire
anemone

Actinia
anemone

Bubble
anemone

Oil Spill Awareness

On March 24, 1989, a huge oil tanker sailed out of the port of Valdez, Alaska. When the Exxon-Valdez crashed into an underwater reef, it released millions of gallons of thick, black oil into the dark water. *Oil Spill!* by Melvin Berger, illustrated by Paul Mirocha (HarperCollins, 1994), describes the Exxon-Valdez accident, and includes ways to help prevent spills, including using less oil!

Materials:

"Letter to Senator" Hands-on Handout (p. 45), *Oil Spill!* (or other book on oil spills—see "Nonfiction Resources" at the back of this book), "Super-Duper Fact Card" on oil (p. 73)

Directions:

1. Duplicate the "Letter to Senator" Hands-on Handout for each child.
2. Read *Oil Spill!* with the class, or duplicate the "Super-Duper Fact Card" on oil for each child.
3. Discuss what happens when an oil spill occurs.
4. Have your students help compile a list of fish and animals that are hurt when there's an oil spill. Write this list on the chalkboard.
5. Have students brainstorm ways to prevent oil spills in the future. Write these methods on the chalkboard.
6. Let the children fill in the letter form on the "Letter to Senator" Hands-on Handout. Older students might want to write their own letters. Younger students might work together in teams to fill in the form.
7. Mail the letters to your senator, representative, or an oil company CEO.

Letter to Senator

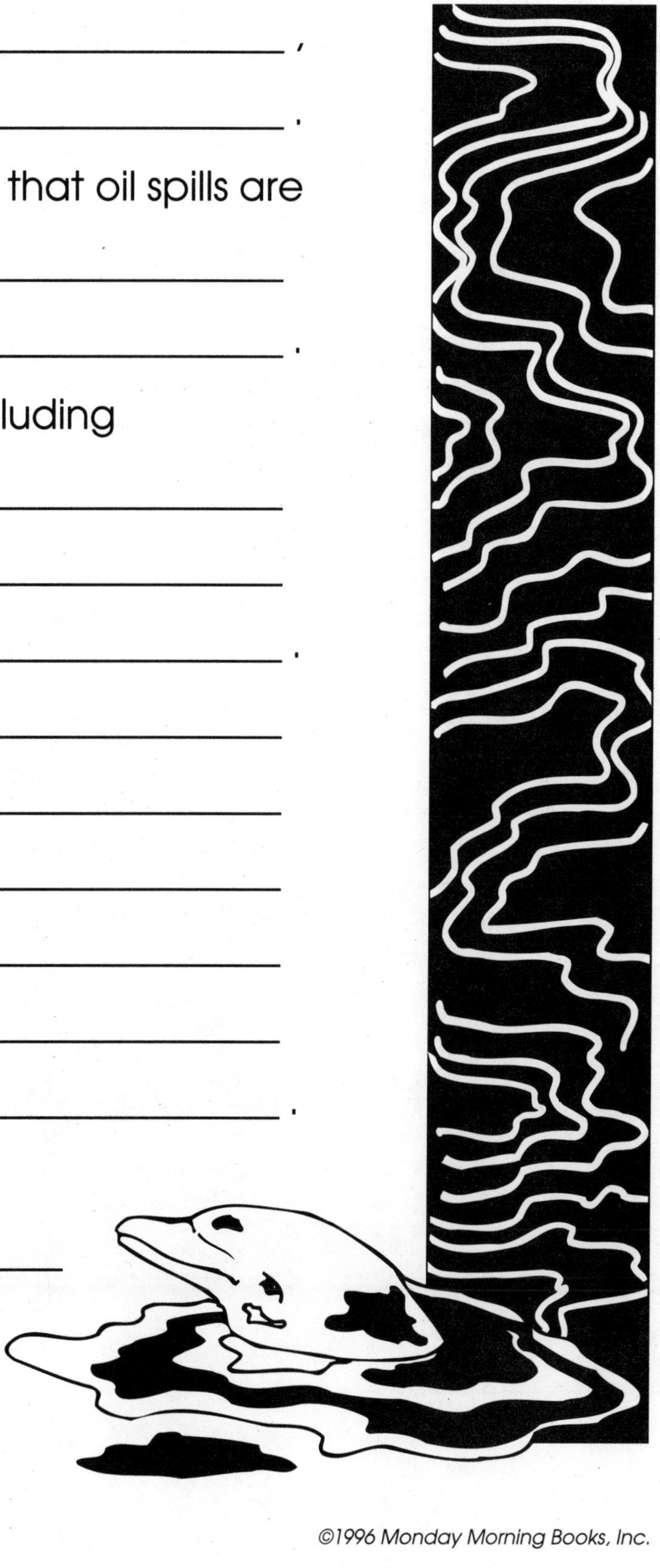

Dear Senator _____ ,

My name is _____ .

I am in _____ grade. I think that oil spills are

_____

_____ .

Oil spills hurt many animals, including

_____

_____

_____ .

To prevent oil spills, we should _____

_____

_____

_____

_____ .

Sincerely,

_____

Ocean Mobile Report

Materials:
"Ocean Patterns" (pp. 48-49), "Ocean Facts" Hands-on Handout (p. 47), "Super-Duper Fact Cards" (pp. 70-77), nonfiction ocean books, heavy oaktag or tag board, scissors, construction paper, hole punch, yarn, hangers, pens or pencils, crayons or markers, glitter, glue

Directions:
1. Divide your students into groups of five or six.
2. Each child in the group should learn two facts about a creature that lives in the ocean. The children can choose creatures from the ocean patterns.
3. Children can use the "Super-Duper Fact Cards," or do research on their own using books in the library. Have children write their facts on the "Ocean Facts" Hands-on Handout. They will use their facts to make visual reports by creating cooperative mobiles.
4. Duplicate and enlarge the "Ocean Patterns" onto heavy oak tag or tagboard.
5. Children should write the facts on the back of the patterns so that the facts can be read when the mobiles turn.
6. Provide decorative materials for children to use to decorate the patterns.
7. Help children punch holes in the patterns, thread through with yarn, and fasten the yarn to hangers.
8. Hang the completed mobiles in the classroom or in the school library.

Ocean Facts

Name: _____

Date: _____

My fact 1:

_____

_____

My fact 2:

_____

_____

Books I used:

Title: _____

Author: _____

Title: _____

Author: _____

Title: _____

Author: _____

Ocean Patterns

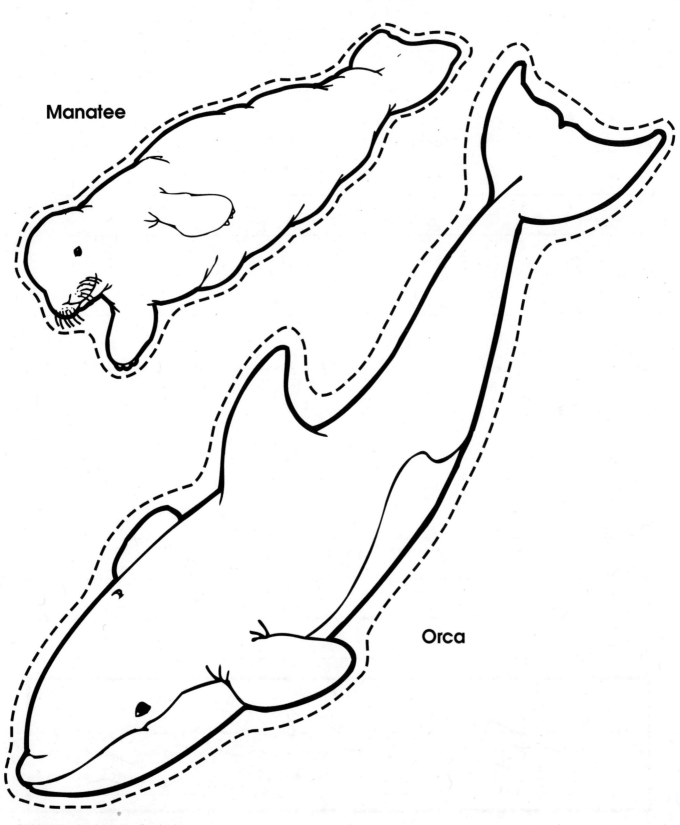

Manatee

Orca

Ocean Patterns

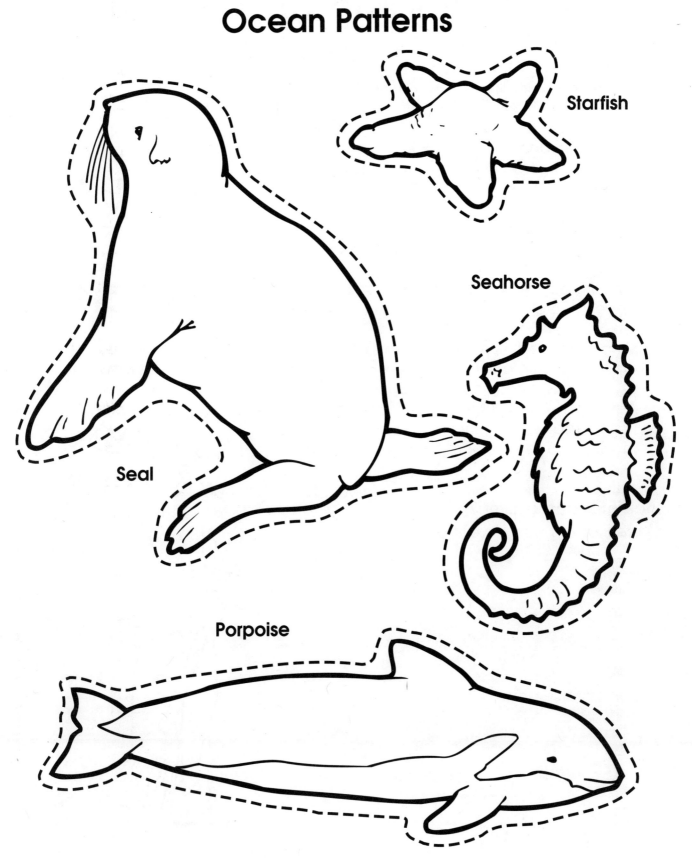

Starfish

Seahorse

Seal

Porpoise

The Walrus and the Carpenter

Story:

The Walrus and the Carpenter by Lewis Carroll, illustrated by Jane Breskin Zalben (Holt, 1986).
This poem, originally published in 1871 in *Through the Looking Glass, and What Alice Found There*, is a delicious nonsense romp that children will undoubtedly love!

Setting the Stage:

- Create an oyster bed on the bulletin board. Post small paper plate "oysters" with drawn-on faces on a board backed with green and blue construction paper. (The children can help you create this display.)
- Bring child-sized mops into the classroom for children to use to pretend to be "seven maids with seven mops" sweeping the seashore clean.
- Serve bread and butter while you read the poem. Eat the snack picnic-style, on a blanket spread on the floor of the classroom (or outside in the yard, if possible).

Tricky Tongue Twister:

Oysters aren't noisy, are they?

The Walrus's Poetry Hour

Materials:
"The Walrus and the Carpenter" poem (pp. 52-53), highlighter pen

Directions:
1. Duplicate the poem for each child.
2. Have each child learn part of the poem (either two or four lines, depending on the ability of your students).
3. Use a highlighter pen to highlight the part on his or her poem that each child is going to learn.
4. Host a classroom poetry hour, and have each child perform, stating the memorized lines. (Children who can't remember their lines can read the lines from note cards.)

Option 1:
Invite other classes or parents and guardians to listen to your poetry hour.

Option 2:
Have children dress in simple costumes while they perform. They can make paper bag costumes and paper plate masks.

The sun was shining on the sea, shining with all his might...

The Walrus and the Carpenter

The sun was shining on the sea,
Shining with all his might:
He did his very best to make
The billows smooth and bright—
And this was odd, because it was
The middle of the night.

The moon was shining sulkily,
Because she thought the sun
Had got no business to be there
After the day was done—
"It's very rude of him," she said,
"To come and spoil the fun!"

The sea was wet as wet could be,
The sands were dry as dry.
You could not see a cloud because
No cloud was in the sky:
No birds were flying overhead—
There were no birds to fly.

The Walrus and the Carpenter
Were walking close at hand:
They wept like anything to see
Such quantities of sand:
"If this were only cleared away,"
They said, "it would be grand!"

"If seven maids with seven mops
Swept it for half a year,
Do you suppose," the Walrus said,
"That they could get it clear?"
"I doubt it," said the Carpenter,
And shed a bitter tear.

"O Oysters, come and walk with us!"
The Walrus did beseech.
"A pleasant walk, a pleasant talk,
Along the briny beach:
We cannot do with more than four,
To give a hand to each."

The eldest Oyster looked at him,
But never a word he said:
The eldest Oyster winked his eye,
And shook his heavy head—
Meaning to say he did not choose
To leave the oyster-bed.

But four young Oysters hurried up,
All eager for the treat:
Their coats were brushed, their
    faces washed,
Their shoes were clean and neat—
And this was odd, because,
    you know,
They hadn't any feet.

Four other Oysters followed them,
And yet another four;
And thick and fast they came at last,
And more, and more, and more—
All hopping through the frothy waves,
And scrambling to the shore.

The Walrus and the Carpenter
Walked on a mile or so,
And then they rested on a rock
Conveniently low:
And all the little Oysters stood
And waited in a row.

"The time has come," the Walrus
    said,
"To talk of many things:
Of shoes—and ships—and sealing-
    wax—
Of cabbages—and kings—
And why the sea is boiling hot—
And weather pigs have wings."

"But wait a bit," the Oysters cried,
"Before we have our chat;
For some of us are out of breath,
And all of us are fat!"
"No hurry!" said the Carpenter.
They thanked him much for that.

"A loaf of bread," the Walrus said,
"Is what we chiefly need:
Pepper and vinegar besides
Are very good indeed—
Now, if you're ready, Oysters dear,
We can begin to feed."

"But not on us!" the Oysters cried,
Turning a little blue.
"After such kindness, that would be
A dismal thing to do!"
"The night is fine," the Walrus said.
"Do you admire the view?"

"It was so kind of you to come!
And you are very nice!"
The Carpenter said nothing but
"Cut us another slice.
I wish you were not quite so deaf—
I've had to ask you twice!"

"It seems a shame," the Walrus said,
"To play them such a trick.
After we've brought them out so far,
And made them trot so quick!"
The Carpenter said nothing but
"The butter's spread too thick!"

"I weep for you," the Walrus said:
"I deeply sympathize."
With sobs and tears he sorted out
Those of the largest size,
Holding his pocket-handkerchief
Before his streaming eyes.

"O Oysters," said the Carpenter,
"You've had a pleasant run!
Shall we be trotting home again?"
But answers came there none—
And this was scarcely odd, because
They'd eaten every one.

The Owl and the Pussycat

Story:

The Owl and the Pussy-cat by Edward Lear, illustrated by Paul Galdone (Clarion, 1987).
The owl and the pussycat take a magnificent journey in a pea-green boat. They land on an island, where they get married and dance "by the light of the moon."

Setting the Stage:

- Play waltz music in the classroom and let children pair off and dance together. (Or they can dance alone.)
- Cut a large full moon shape from yellow or white paper and post it on a bulletin board. Add a few silver stars (cardboard star shapes covered in aluminum foil). You might even hang these from a clothesline strung across the classroom.
- Bring in an inflatable rubber raft for children to take turns sitting in while you read the story.
- Play a guitar (or recorded guitar music).
- Serve crackers and honey (which the owl and the pussycat snacked on).

Tricky Tongue Twister:

See them sail the sea in a sailboat.

The Owl and the Pussycat

Materials:
Butcher paper, tempera paints, paintbrushes, newsprint, pencils

Directions:
1. After reading this story, let children draw a larger-than-life illustration for it.
2. Cover the work area with newsprint.
3. Spread the butcher paper over the newsprint.
4. Let children use tempera paints and brushes to illustrate the mural. (They can plan it out ahead of time and sketch with pencils where they want the objects to go.)
5. Children can add other sea creatures, plants, and animals that they've learned about. Help them label the items on the mural.
6. Once the mural has dried, post it in the classroom or in the library. You might set up several illustrated versions of this story, including *Albert's Play* by Leslie Tryon (Atheneum, 1992).

The Great White Man-Eating Shark

Story:

The Great White Man-Eating Shark: A Cautionary Tale by Margaret Mahy, pictures by Jonathan Allen (Dial, 1990).

Norvin wishes he had the cove where he swims all to himself. He decides to pretend to be a shark, scaring off the other swimmers. Finally, he is happily alone...at least until he is discovered by a love-struck female shark!

Setting the Stage:

- Let children make Valentines that are from the shark to Norvin. Post these on a "Love-struck Shark" bulletin board.
- Use blue crepe paper to make a wave border on your walls. Cut out grey triangles to represent the frightening shark fins.
- Hold a dental-awareness week, and post floss containers, toothbrushes, and smile reminders on the bulletin board.
- Cut out small triangles and punch a hole in each one. Let children string the triangles onto yarn and wear as "shark tooth" good luck necklaces.

Tricky Tongue Twister:

The swiftly swimming sea shark smiled.

A Tooth Fairy's Tale

Materials:
Writing paper, pencils, drawing paper, crayons or markers, "Shark Tooth Pattern" (p. 33)

Directions:
1. Have your children imagine that they are tooth fairies.
2. Provide writing paper and have the children write short stories about retrieving a shark's tooth (from under its seaweed pillow) and leaving a prize. Ask them to think about the size of the tooth and what they would leave the shark (something the shark might think was really special).
3. Let children illustrate their stories using drawing paper and crayons or markers.
4. Bind the stories in a "Tooth Fairy's Tales" storybook, or post both stories and pictures in the classroom. (Make a border using copies of the shark tooth pattern.)

The Night of the Moonjellies

Story:

The Night of the Moonjellies by Mark Shasha (Simon & Schuster, 1992).

Seven-year-old Mark helps his grandmother and other family members run their seaside hot dog stand. One day, he finds a surprise on the beach, a strange creature. That night, Gran takes Mark on a special boat ride, to witness the night of the moonjellies. (See page 11 for a picture of a moonjelly.)

Setting the Stage:

- Make a batch of clear gelatin and let it "gel" in clear plastic bags tied tightly. Place these on counters (on top of paper plates) around the class room for effect while you read the story.
- Let children create special "keepsake" boxes. Provide plain cardboard boxes (with lids) in assorted shapes and sizes. Have children glue shell-shaped pasta and other textured items to the boxes. Take the boxes outside and spray-paint them using gold or silver paint. (Do this when there are no children present.) Once the boxes have dried, your students can take them home.
- Host a weenie (or hot dog) roast at lunch time. Invite parents and guardians, or children from other classes.

Tricky Tongue Twister:

I giggle when my moonjelly jiggles.

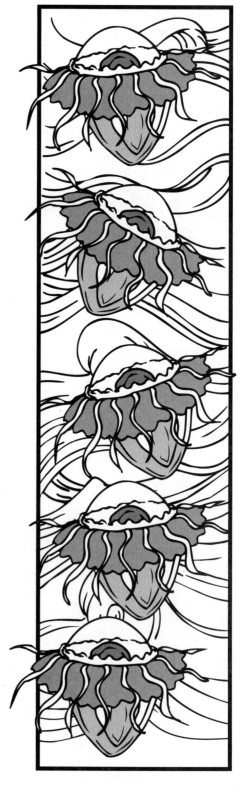

Shake Just Like a Bowl of . . . Moonjellies

Materials:
Chalkboard, chalk

Directions:
1. Write the descriptive starters on the bottom of this page on the chalkboard. (These are only samples. You can create more.)
2. Let students take turns completing the phrases.
3. Host a day when children use only ocean words—names of ocean creatures and plants, and descriptions of ocean environments—to describe things. For example, they might say they were "happier than a hermit crab in its new home." Or "slower than a giant clam closing its shell." Or "more uncomfortable than an oyster making a pearl."

Faster than a . . .
Bigger than a . . .
Meaner than a . . .
Tougher than a . . .
Sneakier than a . . .
Smaller than a . . .
Older than a . . .
Slower than a . . .
Duller than a . . .

Slower than a clam
closing its shell.

Treasure Chest Stories

Materials:
"Treasure Chest Pattern" (p. 61), pencils or pens, crayons or markers, hole punch, yarn, tagboard or oak tag

Directions:
1. When Mark goes to "work" at the hot dog stand in *The Night of the Moonjellies*, he finds a moonjelly on the beach. Later that night, his grandmother shows him the magic of moonjellies. Have your students imagine finding some natural "treasure" on the beach.
2. Duplicate the treasure pattern for each child in the class, plus make two extra copies on thick tagboard or oak tag.
3. Have the children write a short story about their treasure in the "Treasure Chest Pattern" and draw a picture in the top of the treasure chests.
4. Bind the stories in a classroom "Treasure Album." Make a cover for the book using the patterns duplicated onto heavy paper. Punch two holes in each page and bind together with yarn.
5. Display the book in your classroom.

Treasure Chest Pattern

Outstanding Oceans Program

Songs:
- Bozo the Clownfish
- Do You Have a Spout?
- I Once Saw a Shark
- A Pirate Chant
- The Old Pirate Song
- Jellyfish Rock
- I'm a Seahorse
- Tidal Pool

Featuring:

Bozo the Clownfish

(to the tune of "Frosty, the Snowman)

Bozo, the clownfish,
Is a clown beneath the sea—
He can make you grin
With his cool, striped fins
As he waves to you and me!

Bozo, the clownfish,
Is a fish you've got to see—
He can keep things neat
As he eats and eats
'Round the sea anemones.

(chorus)
When Bozo swims the other fish
All follow him around.
He entertains them with his games
And by acting like a clown!

Bozo, the clownfish,
Is a clown you've got to see!
He will make you grin
With his cool, striped fins
As he waves to you and me!

Do You Have a Spout?

(to the tune of "You're a Grand Old Flag")

Do you have a spout?
Do you spout water out?
Do you sing to your friends in the sea?
Is a seaweed treat, a meal you'd eat,
And plankton a great specialty?

When you flip your tail,
Do you call other whales,
And do all of your friends swim by?
And when all your friends flip all their tails,
Are you proud to be a blue whale?

I Once Saw a Shark

(to the tune of "Home on the Range")

I once saw a shark,
When I swam after dark,
It was big, with a frightening grin.
Its teeth were quite white,
They shined in the moonlight,
And it had a triangular fin.

Shark, you can't fool me.
'Cause I've heard from the fish in the sea.
And I've got a hunch
I'll wind up as your lunch,
Which is not something I want to be!

A Pirate Chant

Ahoy there, matey!
What will you say
On the day that I capture your boat?
Will you tell by my flag
(With the skull and the bones)
Or the dagger that's under my coat?

Will you try to escape,
Or give up your gold,
Will you struggle or just come along?
What will you say, my young sailing
   chum,
When I teach you the Old Pirate Song?

The Old Pirate Song

(to the tune of "Oh, Susannah")

Hey, there, matey!
Now, don't you cry for me,
For a pirate's life is filled with such
Adventure on the sea!

It may rain hard,
The waves may crash,
My boat might not behave.
But, oh, I love my pirate life,
At sea among the waves.

Hey, there, matey!
Now, don't you cry for me,
For a pirate's life is filled with such
Adventure on the sea!

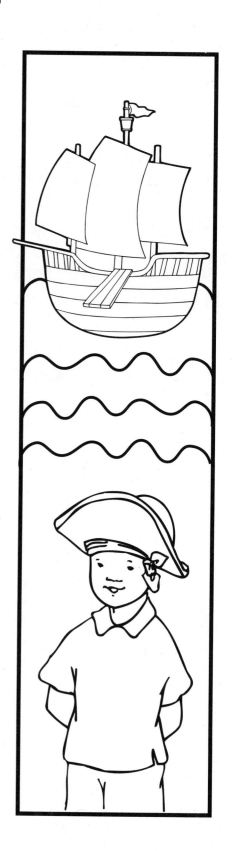

Jellyfish Rock

(to the tune of "Jingle Bell Rock")

Jellyfish, jellyfish, jellyfish swim.
Jellyfish float on jellyfish waves.
Jellyfish dance in their jellyfish way.
Watch them swish and sway.

Jellyfish, jellyfish, jellyfish glide,
Jellyfish go on jellyfish rides.
Jellies can wiggle, jellies can float,
They're like little boats.

Oh, a jelly's quite a creature,
It's got tentacles, too.
It starts glowing in the night sky,
Looking pretty for me and for you.

Jellyfish, jellyfish, jellyfish swim.
Jellyfish float on jellyfish waves.
Jellyfish dance in their jellyfish way.
Watch them swish and sway!

I'm a Seahorse

(to the tune of "Alouette")

I'm a seahorse,
Yes, I am a seahorse.
I'm a seahorse,
I live in the sea.
I suck shrimp through my long nose.
It works sort of like a hose.
My long nose,
My long nose,
Like a hose,
Like a hose.
Ahhhh...
I'm a seahorse,
Yes, I am a seahorse.
I'm a seahorse,
I live in the sea.

Tidal Pool

(to the tune of "Jingle Bells")

Barnacles, sugar kelp, sea anemones,
Animals and plant life, friends and enemies.
Look, here comes a rock crab,
Trying to stay cool.
This is what you'll find
When you study tidal pools.

Limpets on the sides, sea stars on the floor,
Kelp and tiny fish, wait, there's even more.
Algae floating by, prawns here by the bunch,
Now here comes a gull,
Looking for some lunch.

Barnacles, sugar kelp, sea anemones,
Animals and plant life, friends and enemies.
Look, here comes a rock crab,
Trying to stay cool.
This is what you'll find
When you study tidal pools.

Coral Reef Facts

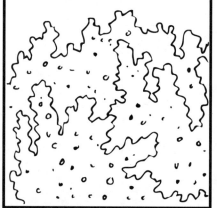

Habitat: Most corals live in large groups or colonies. The skeletons of the corals build up into huge underwater reefs.

Home: Coral reefs provide a home for many different marine creatures. Some creatures feed on the corals. Others hunt the small fish and shellfish that live near the reef.

Super-Duper Fact: Some coral colonies may be as much as 500 million years old!

Fish Facts

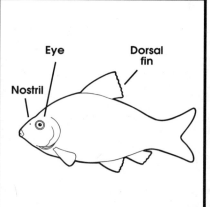

Eye

Dorsal fin

Nostril

Habitat: Some fish, such as tuna, live in the open sea. Many small fish live near the shore.

Food: Little fish eat plants, plankton, and tiny sea animals. Small fish are eaten by medium-sized fish. Big fish eat the medium-sized fish and the small fish.

Babies: Some fish give birth to live young.

Super-Duper Fact: The largest fish is called the whale shark.

Giant Clam Facts

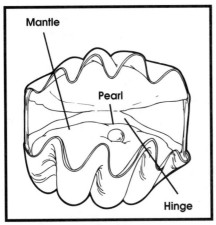

Habitat: Most giant clams are found in the South Pacific. Giant clams may live to be over 150 years old!

Enemies: When danger is present, the giant clam closes its shell. But don't worry—a diver couldn't get stuck inside. The shell closes very, very slowly.

Super-Duper Fact: The largest giant clam on record weighed more than 500 pounds.

Jellyfish Facts

Habitat: Jellyfish can be found in the open seas. Almost all jellyfish live in saltwater.

Food: A jellyfish uses its long tentacles to catch food. Once it holds a fish, it stings the fish with poison. Then the fish cannot swim and the jellyfish eats it.

Super-Duper Fact: Many jellyfish give off light to attract prey or mates or to light their own way.

Moray Eel Facts

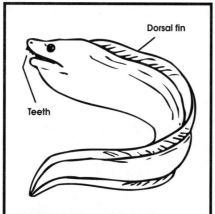

Habitat: Moray eels live in coral holes. They have long bodies that let them fit into tight places.
Food: These eels eat fish, crabs, and lobster. An eel can eat an octopus! Eels hunt at night.
Enemies: Some enemies are the snapper and the grouper.
Breathing: Moray eels open and close their mouths to breathe.
Super-Duper Fact: Moray eels can grow to be eight feet long.

Octopus Facts

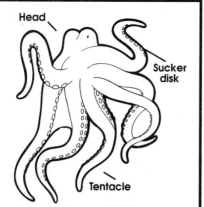

Habitat: Octopuses live in oceans all over the world. Octopuses often live in caves.
Food: Octopuses eat crabs, lobsters, and shrimp.
Enemies: Octopuses confuse their enemies by squirting ink at them.
Babies: Octopus moms lay their eggs in long strands attached to the ceiling of their caves.
Super-Duper Fact: Baby octopuses can change color and squirt ink even before they hatch!

Oil Facts

Location: Much of the oil and natural gas we use is pumped from ocean floors.

Origin: Oil and gas were formed millions of years ago. Both are made from the decayed bodies of dead plants and animals.

Problems: When there are oil spills, the oil can harm both plants and animals that live in the sea.

Super-Duper Fact: When the Exxon-Valdez hit an underwater reef, it spilled enough oil to fill 1,000 pools!

Porpoise Facts

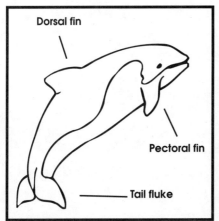

Dorsal fin

Pectoral fin

Tail fluke

Habitat: Porpoises are found in all oceans.

Food: Porpoises eat fish.

Enemies: Sometimes porpoises can get trapped in fishing nets.

How they "talk": The porpoise speaks by air moving through its blowhole.

Babies: Porpoises are mammals. They nurse their young.

Super-Duper Fact: Porpoises breathe air, just like you.

Sea Anemone Facts

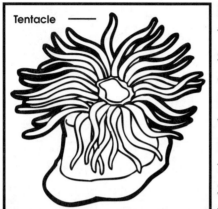

Tentacle

Habitat: Anemones can attach themselves to the bottom of the sea, or to seaweed, jellyfish, coral, or even a crab's shell.
Food: Anemones eat crabs, worms, and fish.
Relatives: Anemones are related to jellyfish.
Size: Most sea anemones are a few inches long. Some are bigger.
Super-Duper Fact: Clownfish and damselfish live among the anemones' tentacles. They clean up for the anemones.

Sea Cucumber Facts

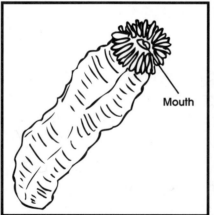

Mouth

Habitat: Sea cucumbers can be found in all oceans.
Enemies: Sea cucumbers defend themselves by turning inside out and spewing out their inside organs!
Length: Sea cucumbers are usually the size of real cucumbers, less than one foot (30.5 cm).
Super-Duper Fact: It takes about six weeks before the sea cucumber can regrow its inside organs.

Seahorse Facts

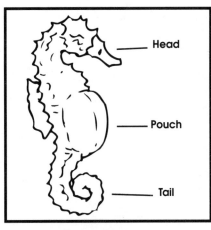

Habitat: Seahorses are usually found in shallow waters.
Food: Seahorses suck up shrimp with their long noses.
Enemies: Seahorses hide from enemies by camouflage.
Babies: The mother lays the eggs. The father seahorse carries the eggs in a pouch on his front.

Super-Duper Fact: Seahorses have little fins on the sides of their heads (where ears would be) to help them change direction.

Sea Slug Facts

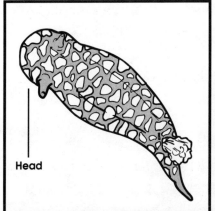

Habitat: Sea slugs can be found in oceans all over the world.
Food: Sea slugs can eat animals that sting. The stinging cells don't bother them.
Enemies: Sea slugs are covered with slime that tastes bad to their enemies.
Babies: Sea slug babies have shells. Adult slugs do not.

Super-Duper Fact: Sea slugs are usually brightly colored. They are colored by what they eat.

Shark Facts

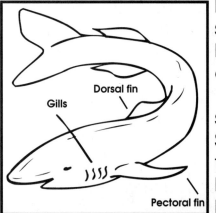

Habitat: Sharks can be found in all seas. They prefer warm waters.
Food: Many sharks are meat eaters. The white shark is called "the man-eater." It attacks swimmers and boats.
Size: Sharks range in size from 2 feet to 50 feet!
Babies: Sharks give birth to live babies, not eggs.
Super-Duper Fact: Sharks could not survive without their sharp teeth. The blue shark has spare teeth.

Starfish Facts

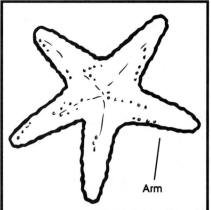

Habitat: Starfish can be found on many beaches, just below the tide line.
Food: Starfish use tentacles to trap clams, snails, and mussels. They drill through a clam's shell with their chisel-like mouth parts.
Confusing the enemy: Some starfish can break off an arm at will and grow a new one.
Super-Duper Fact: Starfish have no back or front. This means that they can move in any direction they like.

Tide Pool Facts

Habitat: Tide pools are areas on beaches that are protected by rocks.

Home: Starfish, crabs, prawns, plants, and fish live in tide pools.

How: The tide washes water, plants, and animals into the tide pool every day. It sweeps out some of the plants and animals living in the pool.

Super-Duper Fact: Tide pools change every time the tide comes in.

Whale Facts

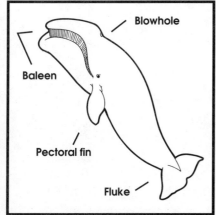

Blowhole

Baleen

Pectoral fin

Fluke

Fish or mammal? Whales are mammals. This means that they nurse their young.

Way of breathing: Whales have a blowhole on the top of their heads.

Way of "talking": Whales "talk" by using sounds. They can hear over great distances. They talk in different ways to males or females.

Super-Duper Fact: Some whales can stay underwater for up to two hours.

Ocean A to Z List

A: Abalone, Anchovy, Ark Shell
B: Barracuda, Brain Coral, Blue Whale
C: Clam, Clownfish, Coral, Crab, Cuttlefish
D: Dolphin
E: Eel
F: Feather Duster Worm, Fiddler Crab, Fireworm
G: Giant Squid, Goby, Great White Shark, Grunt
H: Hammerhead Shark, Hermit Crab, Herring
I: Indian Ocean, Island, Ichthyology
J: Jack Fish, Jellyfish, Jingle Shell
K: Kelp, Killer Whale
L: Leatherback Turtle, Limpet, Lobster
M: Manatee, Moray Eel, Mussel
N: Nut Clam
O: Oar Fish, Octopus, Osprey (ocean-going bird)
P: Pearl, Periwinkle, Plankton, Porpoise, Prawn
Q: Queen Trigger Fish
R: Rattail Fish, Razor Clam, Razor Shell, Reef
S: Sand Dollar, Sea Slug, Seahorse, Shark, Squid
T: Tube Sponge, Tunic (also called "Sea Squirt")
U: Urchin
V: Volcano
W: Walrus, Whelk (shell), Whorl-forming Coral
X: Xancus angulatus (West Indian Chank Shell)
Y: Yellowfin Tuna
Z: Zooplankton

Xancus angulatus

Nonfiction Resources

- *Coral* by Francine Jacobs, illustrated by D. D. Tyler (G. P. Putnam's Sons, 1980).
- *Corals: The Sea's Great Builders* by the Cousteau Society (Simon & Schuster, 1992).
- *Discovering Seashells* by Douglas Florian (Scribner's, 1986).
- *Exploring the Sea: Oceanography Today* by Carvel Hall Blair, Ph.D., illustrated by Harry McNaughty (Random House, 1986).
- *Exploring the Seashore* by William H. Amos (National Geographic, 1984).
- *Eyewitness Books: Shark* by Miranda MacQuitty (Dorling Kindersley, 1992).
- *Going on a Whale Watch* by Bruce McMillan (Scholastic, 1992).
- *Hungry Sharks* by John F. Waters, illustrated by Ann Dalton (Thomas Y. Crowell, 1973).
- *I Am the Ocean* by Suzanna Marshak, illustrated by James Endicott (Arcade, 1991).
- *Life on a Coral Reef* by Lionel Bender (Glocester, 1989).
- *Moon Jelly Swims Through the Sea* by Marie M. Jenkins, illustrated by Rene Martin (Holiday House, 1969). Part of the life-cycle series.
- *Sharks* by John Bonnett Wexo (Creative Education, 1989).
- *Sharks, the Super Fish* by Helen Roney Sattler, illustrated by Jean Day Zallinger (Lothrop, Lee & Shepard, 1986).
- *Tentacles: The Amazing World of Octopus, Squid, and Their Relatives* by James Martin (Crown, 1993).
- *Wonders of Corals and Coral Reefs* by Morris K. Jacobson & David R. Franz (Dodd, 1979).
- *Wonders of the World of Shells: Sea, Land and Fresh-Water* by Morris K. Jacobson and William K. Emerson (Dodd, 1971).
- *The World of a Jellyfish* by David Shale and Jennifer Coldrey, photographs by Oxford Scientific Films (Gareth Stevens, 1987).

Additional Resources

A Field Trip to the Bottom of the Sea!

The Smithsonian is unveiling a new sea-themed exhibit called "Ocean Planet." The exhibit is made up of several sections, including Ocean Science (where visitors receive an introduction to the exotic life forms, landscapes, and environments in the oceans), Sea Store (which focuses on the many products and services that people depend on from the sea), Ocean in Peril (where visitors learn about threats to marine habitats, such as pollution and over-fishing), and Sea Theater (which stages short plays about the oceans). "Ocean Planet" also includes:

- A 30-foot walkway that gives visitors all the sights and sounds of plunging into the ocean, as if on a wave;
- A computer-generated tour beneath the Pacific; and
- A video of a submarine research expedition.

The exciting exhibit explores the amazing world of the oceans while also documenting the risks associated with pollution.

The mobile exhibit will be touring Washington, D.C., New York, Baltimore, Boston, Chicago, Los Angeles, and several other cities.

Dolphin Log
The Cousteau Society
870 Greenbrier Circle
Suite 402
Chesapeake, VA 23320

This magazine for youngsters is filled with color photos, activities, and amazing facts about the sea. Subscriptions are available for $10 a year.